ONE HUNDRED MORE POEMS
FROM THE JAPANESE

by

KENNETH REXROTH

A NEW DIRECTIONS BOOK

ACKNOWLEDGMENTS

Some of the material in this book first appeared in *New Directions in Prose and Poetry 29* and Kenneth Rexroth's *New Poems* (New Directions, 1974).

I am deeply grateful to Morita Yasuyo who went over my translations with me, line by line, and to Kodama Sanehide who did also and who read the proof on the *romaij* with great care. Any mistakes or controversial translations are my own. This book, along with several others, was done on a Fulbright Fellowship in 1974–75. I wish to express my gratitude for the helpfulness of their Tokyo staff and especially Ms. Yamaguchi Toyoko, and not least to the grantors who specified that the grant was "to write poetry." — K. R.

Manufactured in the United States of America
New Directions Books are printed on acid-free paper.
First published clothbound and as New Directions Paperbook 420 in 1976
Published simultaneously in Canada by Penguin Books Canada Limited

Library of Congress Cataloging in Publication Data

One hundred more poems from the Japanese.

  (A New Directions Book)
  Includes bibliographical references.
  1. Japanese poetry — Translations into English.
  2. English poetry — Translations from Japanese.
  1. Rexroth, Kenneth, 1905 –
PL782.E305   895.6'1'008   76–7486
ISBN 0–8112–0618–1
ISBN 0–8112–0619–X pbk.

New Directions Books are published for James Laughlin by New Directions Publishing Corporation, 80 Eighth Avenue, New York 10011

ELEVENTH PRINTING

TABLE OF CONTENTS

FOR CAROL

ONE HUNDRED MORE POEMS
FROM THE JAPANESE

I

The black jewel like
Night grows late.
Where the hisagi trees
Overhang the pure white
River beach like a roof
The plovers wail again and again.

Nubatama no
Yo no fukeyukeba
Hisagi ouru
Kiyoki kawara ni
Chidori shiba naku

YAMABE NO AKAHITO

II

In Waka Bay when
The tide covers the sand bars
The cranes fly across
To the reeds of the other
Shore, making great cries.

Waka no ura ni
Shio michi kureba
Kata wo nami
Ashibe wo sashite
Tazu naki wataru

YAMABE NO AKAHITO

山
部
赤
人

III

Amidst the notes
Of my koto is another
Deep mysterious tone,
A sound that comes from
Within my own breast.

> *Koto no ne ni*
> *Kyosho no oto no*
> *Uchi majiru*
> *Kono ayashisa mo*
> *Mune no hibiki zo*

YOSANO AKIKO

与
謝
野
晶
子

IV

At the beginning
Of the night the whispering
Snow fell, and now stars
Fill this world below on the
Dishevelled hair about my face.

Yoru no cho ni
Sasameki tsukishi
Hoshi no ima wo
Gekai no hito no
Bin no hotsure yo

YOSANO AKIKO

V

Black hair
Tangled in a thousand strands.
Tangled my hair and
Tangled my tangled memories
Of our long nights of love making.

Kuro kami no
Chi suji no kami no
Midaregami
Katsu omoimidare
Omoimidaruru

YOSANO AKIKO

VI

Come at last to this point
I look back on my passion
And realize that I
Have been like a blind man
Who is unafraid of the dark.

Ima koko ni
Kaerimi sureba
Waga nasake
Yami o osorenu
Meshii ni nitari

YOSANO AKIKO

VII

Hair unbound, in this
Hothouse of lovemaking,
Perfumed with lilies,
I dread the oncoming of
The pale rose of the end of night.

Taki-gami ni
Muro mutsumaji no
Yuri no kaori
Kie o ayabumi
Yo no toki-iro yo

YOSANO AKIKO

VIII

He tempted me to
Come in to say goodbye.
I hesitated to respond
And he brushed my hand away.
But yet — the smell of his clothes
In the soft darkness.

Sasoi irete
Saraba to
Waga te harai masu
Mikeshi no nioi
Yami yawarakaki

YOSANO AKIKO

与
謝
野
晶
子

IX

Left on the beach
Full of water,
A worn out boat
Reflects the white sky
Of early autumn.

Nagisa naru
Sutareshi fune ni
Mizu michite
Shiroku utsureru
Hatsu-aki no sora

YOSANO AKIKO

与謝野晶子

X

Like tiny golden
Birds the ginko leaves scatter
From the tree on the
Hill in the sunset glow.

Konjiki no
Chiisaki tori no
Katachi shite
Ichō chiru nari
Oka no yūhi ni

YOSANO AKIKO

与　謝　野　晶　子

XI

Not speaking of the way,
Not thinking of what comes after,
Not questioning name or fame,
Here, loving love,
You and I look at each other.

Michi o iwazu
Nochi o omowazu
Na o towazu
Koko ni koi kou
Kimi to ware miru

YOSANO AKIKO

XII

Once, far over the breakers,
I caught a glimpse
Of a white bird
And fell in love
With this dream which obsesses me.

Ara iso ni
Tada hito-me mishi
Shiroki tori
Hatsu koi no kimi
Waga yume wa kore

YOSANO AKIKO

与
謝
野
晶
子

XIII

Over the old honeymoon cottage
At the mountain temple
The wild cherry blossoms are falling.
Here, in the desolate false dawn,
The stars go out in heaven.

Yamadera no
Hitoe no sakura
Chiru ni nite
Sabishi yo-ake no
Hoshi kiyuru sora

YOSANO AKIKO

与
謝
野
晶
子

XIV

Press my breasts,
Part the veil of mystery,
A flower blooms there,
Crimson and fragrant.

> *Chibusa osae*
> *Shimpi no tobari*
> *Soto kerinu*
> *Kokonaru hana no*
> *Kurenai zo koki*

YOSANO AKIKO

与
謝
野
晶
子

XV

Swifter than hail,
Lighter than a feather,
A vague sorrow
Crossed my mind.

Arare yori
Hayaku hane yori
Karuyaka ni
Kokoro wa wataru
Awaki kanashimi

YOSANO AKIKO

XVI

That evening when
You went away the two of
Us wrote together
On a pillar a poem
About a white clover.

Kimi yuku to
Sono yūgure ni
Futari shite
Hashira ni someshi
Shirahagi no uta

YOSANO AKIKO

XVII

The uguisu has not come
To sing on this misty day.
Somewhere, I guess, he is sleeping,
His jeweled claws neatly doubled.

Ki-nakanu wo
Kosame furu hi wa
Uguisu mo
Tama-de sashi-kae
Neru ya to omou

YOSANO AKIKO

与謝野晶子

XVIII

This autumn will end.
Nothing can last forever.
Fate controls our lives.
Fondle my living breasts
With your strong hands.

Aki mijikashi
Nani ni fumetsu no
Inochi zo to
Chikara aru chio
Te ni sagurasenu

YOSANO AKIKO

与謝野晶子

XIX

We dressed each other
Hurrying to say farewell
In the depth of night.
Our drowsy thighs touched and we
Were caught in bed by the dawn.

Kinuginu no
Isogu wakare wa
Yo fukakute
Mata ne hisashiki
Akatsuki no toko

THE EMPRESS EIFUKU

永
福
門
院

XX

The plovers cry
Over the evening waves
Of Lake Omi.
In my withering heart
I remember the past.

Ōmi no mi
Yū nami chidori
Na ga nakeba
Kokoro mo shinu ni
Inishie omo oyu

KAKINOMOTO NO HITOMARO

XXI

On the Eastern horizon
Dawn glows over
The fields, and when
I look back I see
The moon setting in the West.

Himukashi no
No ni kagiroi no
Tatsu miete
Kaeri misureba
Tsuki katabukinu

HITOMARO

柿
本
人
麿

XXII

When I gathered flowers
For my girl
From the top of the plum tree
The lower branches
Drenched me with dew.

> *Imo ga tame*
> *Hozu e no ume wo*
> *Ta oru to wa*
> *Shizu e no tsuyu ni*
> *Nurenikeru kamo*

HITOMARO

XXIII

The snow falls and falls.
The mountains and meadows sleep.
Only an old mill
Stays awake.

> *Yuki wa furu furu*
> *Noyama wa nemuru*
> *Hitori nemuranu*
> *Mizu guruma*

ŌKURA ICHIJITSU

XXIV

I picked an azalea
And brought it home.
Now when I contemplate it,
In its crimson dye
I see the color
Of my lover's robe.

Iwa tsutsuji
Orimote zo miru
Seka ga kishi
kurenai some no
Iro ni nitareba

IZUMI SHIKIBU

XXV

In the dusk the path
You used to come to me
Is overgrown and indistinguishable,
Except for the spider webs
That hang across it
Like threads of sorrow.

Yūgure wa
Kimi ga kayoiji
Michi mo naku
Sugakeru kumo no
Ito zo kanashiki

IZUMI SHIKIBU

XXVI

It is the time of rain and snow
I spend sleepless nights
And watch the frost
Frail as your love
Gather in the dawn.

Ame mo furi
Yuki mo furumeru
Kono koro o
Asashimo to nomi
Okiite wa miru

IZUMI SHIKIBU

XXVII

Hey! Ho! Hurrah!
I've got Yasumiko!
The girl they said
Was hard to get!
I've got Yasumiko!

Ware wamoya
Yasumiko etari
Minahito no
Egateni su tou
Yasumiko etari

FUJIWARA NO KAMATARI

XXVIII

Awaji Island—
Back and forth the shore birds go
Crying, calling.
How often in the world,
In the awesome night,
Have they awakened
The guardians of Suma Barrier.

Awajishima
Kayou chidori no
Naku koe ni
Iku yo nezamenu
Suma no sekimori

MINAMOTO NO KANEMASA

XXIX

In the mountain village
The snow falls ceaselessly.
The paths are obliterated.
He would be truly devoted
Who visited me today.

Yamazato wa
Yuki furitsumite
Michi mo nashi
Kyokomu hito wo
Aware to wa mimu

TAIRA NO KANEMORI

XXX

To love somebody
Who doesn't love you,
Is like going to a temple
And worshipping the behind
Of a wooden statue
Of a hungry devil.

Ai omo wan
Hito wo omouwa
Ōdera no
Gaki no shirie ni
Nukazuku gotoshi

LADY KASA YAKAMOCHI

XXXI

Following the roads
Of dream to you, my feet
Never rest. But one glimpse of you
In reality would be
Worth all these many nights of love.

Yumeji ni wa
Ashi mo yasumezu
Kayoedo mo
Utsutsu ni hitome
Mishigoto wa arazu

ONO NO KOMACHI

XXXII

You do not come
On this moonless night.
I wake wanting you.
My breasts heave and blaze.
My heart burns up.

Hito ni awan
Tsuki no naki ni wa
Omoiokite
Mune hashiribi ni
Kokoro yakeori

ONO NO KOMACHI

XXXIII

In the dawn
The white snow falls
Over the village of Yoshino
Like the light
Of the morning moon.

Asaborake
Ariake no tsuki to
Miru made ni
Yoshino no sato ni
Fureru shirayuki

SAKANOE NO KORENORI

XXXIV

This world of ours,
To what shall I compare it?
To the white wake of a boat
That rows away in the early dawn.

> *Yo no naka wo*
> *Nani ni taoemu*
> *Asaborake*
> *Kogi yuku fune no*
> *Ato no shiranami*

SHAMI MANSEI (in the *Shūi Shu*)

XXXV

Who is there? Me.
Me who? I am me, you are you.
But you take my pronoun,
And we are us.

Dare ga iruno? Watashi.
Watashi te dare? Watashi wa watashi,
    anata wa anata.
Demo anata wa watashi ni totte
Futari wa watashitachi ni naru.

MARICHIKO

XXXVI

I wish I could be
Kannon of the thousand heads
To kiss you and Kannon
Of the thousand arms
To embrace you, and
Dainichi to hold you
Forever.

Kannon Bosatsu naraba
Sen no kuchibiru de anata ni kuchizukeshi,
Sen no te de anata wo aibu dekiruno ni,
Soshite Dainichi Nyorai ni natte
Eien ni
Anata wo dakishimete itai.

MARICHIKO

XXXVII

I hold your head tight
Between my thighs and press
Against your mouth and
Float away forever in
An orchid boat
On the River of Heaven.

Anata no atama wo watashi no
Mata ni shikkari hasami
Anata no kuchi ni watashio tsuyoku
Oshitsukeru to, watashi wa
Ran no hana no fune ni notte
Tokoshie ni Tengoku no Kawa wo
Tadayotte yuku.

MARICHIKO

摩利支子

XXXVIII

I cannot forget
The perfumed dusk inside the
Tent of my black hair
As we woke to make love
After a long night of love.

Watashi ni wa wasurerarenai
Nagai ai no yoru no ato
Futatabi ai ni mezameta toki no
Kurokami ni oowarete honoguraku
Kōsui no ka wo todomeru ano temaku wo.

MARICHIKO

XXXIX

Every morning
I wake alone, dreaming
My arm is your sweet flesh
Pressing my lips.

Maiasa mezameruto tada hitori,
Kono ude watashino kuchibiru wo
Oshitsukeru anata no kanbi na
Karada dattano wa yume no naka.

MARICHIKO

XL

Bound up it always
Came undone.
Unbound it was so long.
Now that I have not
Been with you for days
Is your hair all done up?

Takeba nure
Takaneba nagaki
Imo ga kami
Kono goro minuni
Midari tsuramuka

MIKATA SHAMI

三
方
沙
弥

XLI

Everybody tells me
My hair is too long
I leave it
As you saw it last
Dishevelled by your hands.

Hito wa mina
Ima wa nagashito
Taku to iedo
Kimi ga mishi kami
Midare tari tomo

LADY SONO NO OMI IKUHA
(Mikata's wife)

XLII

Ceaseless snow —
No one goes back or forth
Along this road of tears.
No trace remains
Of any sorrow.

Yuki furite
Hito mo kayo wanu
Michi nare ya
Atohaka mo naku
Omoikiyu ramu

ŌSHIKŌCHI NO MITSUNE

XLIII

Spring twilight
Gathers in the mountain village.
As I approach
The cherry petals scatter
At the boom of the evening
Temple bell.

Yamazato no
Haru no yugure
Kite mireba
Iriai no kaneni
Hana zo chirikeri

THE MONK NŌIN

XLIV

Who shall I have for friends,
Now I have grown so old,
That even those ancient companions,
The pines of Takasago,
Are too far away.

Tare wo ka mo
Shiru hito ni semu
Takasago no
Matsu mo mukashi no
Tomo nara naku ni

FUJIWARA NO OKIKAZE

XLV

In the dusk
The road is hard to see.
Wait 'till moonrise,
So I can watch you go.

Yū yami wa
Michi tazutazushi
Tsuki machite
Imase waga seko
Sono ma ni mo mimu

OYAKEME, A GIRL OF BUZEN

XLVI

My heart emptied,
All pity quiet,
Still I am moved, as
A snipe rises and flies away
In the autumn dusk.

Kokoro-naki
Mi nimo aware wa
Shirare keri
Shigi tatsu sawano
Aki no yūgure

SAIGYŌ

XLVII

Why should I be bitter
About someone who was
A complete stranger
Until a certain moment
In a day that has passed.

Utoku naru
Hito wo nanitote
Uramuramu
Shirarezu shiranu
Ori mo arishini

SAIGYŌ

XLVIII

In the spring ravine
In the bright rain
An uguisu begins to sing
In the mountain stillness.

Haru no tani
Akaruki ame no
Nakani shite
Uguisu nakeri
Yama no shizukesa

ONOE NO SHIBAFUNE

XLIX

The crying plovers
On darkening Narumi
Beach, grow closer, wing
To wing, as the moon declines
Behind the rising tide.

> *Sayo chidori*
> *Koe koso chikaku*
> *Narumigata*
> *Katabuku tsuki ni*
> *Shio ya mitsu ramu*

FUJIWARA NO SUEYOSHI

L

Better get drunk and cry
Than show off your learning
In public.

Saka shi mito
Mono yuyori wa
Sake nomi te
Einaki surushi
Masari tarurashi

ŌTOMO NO TABITO

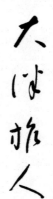

LI

From the beginning
I knew meeting could only
End in parting, yet
I ignored the coming dawn
And I gave myself to you.

Hajime yori
Au wa wakare to
Kikinagara
Akatsuki shirade
Hito o koikeri

FUJIWARA NO TEIKA

LII

I gaze far and long,
Not at cherry blossoms,
Not at autumn leaves,
But at only a thatched hut,
By an inlet,
In the autumn dusk.

Miwataseba
Hana mo momiji mo
Nakarikeri
Ura no tomayano
Aki no yūgure

FUJIWARA NO TEIKA

藤原定家

LIII

I rein in my horse
To shake my sleeves
But there is no shelter
Anywhere near Sano ferry
This snowy evening.

Koma tomete
Sode uchiharo
Kage mo nashi
Sano no watari no
Yuki no yūgure

FUJIWARA NO TEIKA

藤原定家

LIV

The Spring night's
Floating bridge of dreams
Breaks off. The clouds banked
Against the mountain peak
Dissipate in the clear sky.

Haru no yo no
Yume no ukihashi
Todae shite
Mine ni wakareru
Yokogumo no sora

FUJIWARA NO TEIKA

LV

Because
The harvest hut
In the autumn rice field
Was roofed with a coarse grass mat
My sleeves were soaked with dew.

Aki no ta no
Kario no io no
Toma wo arami
Waga koromo de wa
Tsuyu ni nure tsutsu

THE EMPEROR TENCHI

LVI

I remember a grass hut
On a rainy night,
Dreaming of the past,
My tears starting at the cry
Of a mountain cuckoo.

Mukashi omou
Kusa no iori no
Yoru no ame ni
Namida na soe so
Yamahototogisu

FUJIWARA NO TOSHINARI

藤
原
俊
生

LVII

Twilight
The autumn wind on the moor
Penetrates my flesh
The quail cry out
In the deep grass
At Fukakusa village.

Yū sareba
Nobe no akikaze
Mi ni shimite
Uzura naku nari
Fukakusa no sato

FUJIWARA NO TOSHINARI

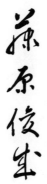

LVIII

I went out in the Spring
To gather the young herbs.
So many petals were falling
Drifting in confused flight
That I lost my way.

Haru no no ni
Wakana tsumamu to
Koshi mono wo
Chiri kō hana ni
Michi wa madoinu

KI NO TSURAYUKI

LIX

When,
Heart overwhelmed with love,
I hurried through the winter night
To the home of my beloved,
The wind on the river was so cold
The plovers cried out in pain.

Omoi kane
Imo gari yukeba
Fuyu no yo no
Kawakaze samumi
Chidori naku nari

KI NO TSURAYUKI

LX

Better never to have met you
In my dream
Than to wake and reach
For hands that are not there.

Ime no ai wa
Kurushi karikeri
Odorokite
Kaki sagure domo
Te ni mo fureneba

ŌTOMO NO YAKAMOCHI
(*to Lady Sakanoe*)

大
は
永
拓

LXI

In the Spring garden
In the colored shadow
Of peach blossoms
A girl stands
On a white path.

Haru no sono
Kurenai niou
Momo no hana
Shita teru michi ni
Ide tatsu otome

ŌTOMO NO YAKAMOCHI

大伴家持

LXII

Over the Spring fields
The haze drifts.
I am sad, pensive.
In this land of the living
As the evening shadows gather,
An uguisu cries
As if in mourning.

Haru no no ni
Kasumi tanabiki
Uraganashi
Kono yūkageni
Uguisu naku mo

ŌTOMO NO YAKAMOCHI

LXIII

The lower leaves of the trees
Tangle the sunset in dusk.
Awe spreads with
The summer twilight.

Hi kurureba
Shitaba koguraki
Ko no moto no
Mono osoroshi ki
Natsu no yūgure

SONE NO YOSHITADA

LXIV

Let us bribe the Moon God
Aloof in high heaven
To make this night as long
As five hundred nights.

Ame ni masu
Tsuku yomi otoko
Mai wa semu
Koyoi no naga sa
Ioyo tsugi koso

PRINCE YUHARA

汤
原
王

LXV

The years have touched me.
I worry that I grow frail with age.
But I only need to see
Your flower like beauty
For all anxiety and heaviness
To leave me.

Toshi fureba
Yowai wa oinu
Shika wa aredo
Hana wo shi mireba
Mono omoi mo nashi

FUJIWARA NO YOSHIFUSA

LXVI

Cloudy morning
The sun dim
I walked in the Palace gardens
And wept where he had walked.

> *Asagumori*
> *Hi no irinureba*
> *Mitatashi no*
> *Shima ni oriite*
> *Nageki tsuru kamo*

ANONYMOUS, *Manyōshū*

LXVII

Her bracelets tinkle
Her anklets clink
She sways at her clattering loom
She hurries to have a new
Obi ready when he comes.

Ashidama mo
Tadama mo yurani
Oru hata wo
Kimi ga mikeshi ni
Nui aemu kamo

ANONYMOUS, *Manyōshū*

LXVIII

On Asuka River
Maple leaves are floating.
On Mount Katsuragi,
High upstream, they are
Already falling from the trees.

Asukagawa
Momiji ba nagaru
Katsuragi no
Yamano konoha wa
Imashi chiru ramu

ANONYMOUS, *Manyōshū*

LXIX

I loathe the twin seas
Of being and not being
And long for the mountain
Of bliss untouched by
The changing tides.

Shoji no
Futatsu no umi wo
Itowashimi
Shiohi no yama wo
Shinubitsuru kamo

ANONYMOUS, *Manyōshū*

LXX

I do not care if
Our love making is exposed
As the rainbow over
The Yasaka dam at Ikaho
If only I can suck and suck you.

Ikahoro no
Yasaka no ide ni
Tatsu nuji no
Arawaro mademo
Sane wo saneteba

ANONYMOUS, *Manyōshū*

LXXI

On Komochi Mountain
From the time the young leaves sprout
Until they turn red
I think I would like to sleep with you
What do you think of that?

Komochiyama
Wakakairude no
Momitsu made
Nemoto wa wa mou
Na wa adoka mou

ANONYMOUS, *Manyōshū*

LXXII

Over the reeds the
Twilight mists rise and settle.
The wild ducks cry out
As the evening turns cold.
Lover, how I long for you.

Ashi no ha ni
Yugiri tachite
Kamo ga ne no
Samuki yube shi
Na woba shinobamu

ANONYMOUS FRONTIER GUARD,
Manyōshū

LXXIII

Shall we stay in the
House to make love, when over
The grasses of Inami Moor
There glows the moonfilled night?

Ie ni shite
Ware wa koimu na
Inami nu no
Asaji ga ue ni
Terishi tsuku yo wo

ANONYMOUS, *Manyōshū*

LXXIV

When I pick up my koto
A cry of sorrow comes from it.
Is it possible that
In the koto's hollow
My wife's spirit
Has secluded itself?

Koto toreba
Nageki sakidatsu
Kedashiku mo
Koto no shitahi ni
Tsuma ya komoreru

ANONYMOUS, *Manyōshū*

LXXV

Until life goes out
Memory will not vanish
But grow stronger
Day by day.

Waga inochi
Mata kemu kagiri
Wasureme ya
Iya hi ni ke ni wa
Omoi masu tomo

ANONYMOUS, *Manyōshū*

LXXVI

Stiff winds blow
At Windy Beach on
Miho Bay. In their row boats
The sailors shout and
Make merry as the surf rises.

Kazahaya no
Miho no urami wo
Kogu fune no
Funabito sawagu
Nami tatsurashi mo

ANONYMOUS, *Manyōshū*

LXXVII

This world of ours,
Before we can know
Its fleeting sorrows,
We enter it through tears.

Yo no naka no
Uki no tsuraki mo
Tsugenaku ni
Mazu shirumono wa
Namida narikeri

ANONYMOUS, *Kokinshū*

LXXVIII

Yoshino River
Flows between Imo Mountain
And Mount Se. All the
World's illusion
Flows between lover and lover.

Nagarete wa
Imo Se no yama no
Naka ni otsuru
Yoshino no kawa no
Yoshiya yo no naka

ANONYMOUS, *Kokinshū*

LXXIX

Evening darkens until
I can no longer see the path.
Still I find my way home,
My horse has gone this way before.

Yūyami wa
Michi mo mienedo
Furusato wa
Moto koshi koma ni
Makasete zo kuru

ANONYMOUS, *Gosenshū*

LXXX

Aching nostalgia —
As evening darkens
And every moment grows
Longer and longer, I feel
Ageless as the thousand year pine.

> *Kururu ma wa*
> *Chitose wo sugusu*
> *Kokochi shite*
> *Matsu wa makoto ni*
> *Hisashikarikeri*

ANONYMOUS, *Goshui Shū*

LXXXI

I cannot go to you
Even in dreams
For in my breast
The skies are overcast
And my mind is clouded.

Yuki yaranu
Yumeji ni madou
Tamoto ni wa
Amatsu sora naki
Tsuyu zo akikeru

ANONYMOUS, *Gosenshū*

LXXXII

Like the tides' flood
In Izumo Bay,
Ever deeper and deeper
Grows my love,
Each time I think of you.

Shio no mitsu
Izumo no ura no
Itsu mo itsu mo
Kimi woba fukaku
Omou wa ya waga

ANONYMOUS

LXXXIII

Our love is infinite
But our nights together
Are very few
How cruel the cock's cry
In the dawn.

Koikoi te
Mare ni au yo no
Akatsuki wa
Tori no netsuraki
Mono ni zarikeru

ANONYMOUS

LXXXIV

The first dawn comes
With a clear bright flicker and
You must go. In the early morning,
We help each other to dress
Trembling with sorrow.

Shinonome no
Hogara – hogara to
Ake yukeba
Ono ga kinu-ginu
Naru zo kanashiku

ANONYMOUS

LXXXV

All day I hoe weeds.
At night I sleep.
All night I hoe again
In dreams the weeds of the day.

> *Nete ruo nemutai*
> *Yoi kara nete mo*
> *Asa no asa kusa*
> *Yume de karu*

ANONYMOUS FOLKSONG

LXXXVI

The cicada cries out
Burning with love.
The firefly burns
With silent love.

Mime de kurushiki
Hi wa taku keredo
Kumuri tataneba
Hito shiranu

ANONYMOUS

LXXXVII

The first time I saw you
Was last year in May,
In May, bathing in a pool
Crowded with iris.

Omae mi someta wa
Kyonen no go gatsu
Go gatsu shobu no
Yu no naka de

ANONYMOUS

LXXXVIII

The moon is full
The night is very still
My heart beats
Like a bell.

Tsuki wa saerushi
Yo wa shin shin to
Kokoro bososa yo
Kane no koe

ANONYMOUS

LXXXIX

The uguisu on the flowering plum,
The stag beneath the autumn maple,
You and me together in bed,
Happy as two fish in the water.

Ume ni uguisu
Momiji ni shika yo
Washi to omae wa
Uo to mizu

ANONYMOUS

XC

We are, you and me,
Like two pine needles
Which will dry and fall
But never separate.

Washi to omae wa
Futa ba no matsu yo
Karete ochite mo
Hanare mai

ANONYMOUS

XCI

When I look at her,
Asleep in the dawn
The body of my girl
Is like a lily
In the field of May.

Sama no ne sugata
Kesa koso mitare
Satsuki no ni saku
Yuri no hana

ANONYMOUS

XCII

My lover, I have lost
Track of time.
What month is it?
Is that an uguisu?
Is this the Spring?

Nushi to tabi surya
Tsuki hi mo wasuru
Uguisu naku so na
Haru ja so na

ANONYMOUS

XCIII

In the summer, by the river,
Let us sit in the evening
And watch the lights of the boats
Caught and confused
In a net of fireflies.

Natsu no yūbe wa
Kawa be no sato ni
Kobune ukabete
Hotaru gari

ANONYMOUS

XCIV

I said in my dream
"Am I dreaming?
Do I dream I dream
This uncanny dream?"

Yume de wa nai ka to
Yume minagara mo
Yume ni yumemiru
Muō na yume

ANONYMOUS

XCV

I dreamed we were back together.
My laughter woke me up.
I searched frantically all around me,
My eyes full of tears.

> *Ōta yume mite*
> *Warō te samete*
> *Atari mimawashi*
> *Namidagumu*

ANONYMOUS

XCVI

Everybody knows
How much I love you.
All your
Mannerisms
Have become my
Mannerisms.

Horeta shōko wa
Omae no kuse ga
Itsu ka watashino
Kuse ni naru

ANONYMOUS

XCVII

Does the bell ring?
Does the beam ring?
The bell and the beam
Ring together.

Kane ga naru ka ye
Shumoku ga naru ka
Kane to shumoku no
Ai ga naru

ANONYMOUS

XCVIII

Did a cuckoo cry?
I open the door
And look out in the garden
There is only the moon
Alone in the night.

Hototogisu kata
Niwa no to akerya
Koyoi no sora nya
Tsuki bakari

ANONYMOUS

XCIX

Clear full moon,
The night is very still.
My heart sounds
Like a bell.

Tsuki wa saerushi
Yo wa shin shin to
Kokoro bososa yo
Kane no koe

ANONYMOUS FOLKSONG

C

A crow caws in the moonlight
I dread the coming dawn
For I have sent away my lover
In tears.

Tsuki yo karasu wo
Yo ake to omoi
Nushi wo kaeshite
Ato kuyamu

ANONYMOUS

CI

I sleep alone,
On my tearstained pillow,
Like an abandoned boat,
Adrift on the sea.

Hitori neru yo wa
Namida no tokono
Fukaki umibe no
Sute obune

ANONYMOUS

CII

When I went with you
To your ship
To say goodbye
My tears choked me
And I said nothing.

Miokurimasho to te
Hama made deta ga
Nakete saraba ga
Ienanda

ANONYMOUS

CIII

In the open sea
With the thousand birds
Crying around me,
How can I ever give up
The life of a sailor?

Oki chidori no
Naku koe kikeba
Funa mori kagyō ga
Yameraryo ka

ANONYMOUS

CIV

I don't care
What anybody says
I will never stop
Loving you.

Hito wa dono yo ni
I ō to mamayo
Tsunorya suru to mo
Yami wa senu

ANONYMOUS

A FEW SAMPLES
OF THE MORE FAMOUS HAIKU

Worshipping at the Great Shrine At Ise —

The tree from whose flower
This perfume comes
Is unknowable.   MATSUO BASHŌ

One plum blossom blooms.
Another blooms.
It grows warmer.   HATTORI RANSETSU

Fields and mountains turn
To shaven monks
Under tonight's moon.   HATTORI RANSETSU

Deep in the night
The River of Heaven
Has completely changed position. HATTORI RANSETSU

Fields and mountains
Have all been taken by the snow.
Nothing is left.   NAITO JŌSŌ

The Autumn cicada
Dies beside its shell.   NAITO JŌSŌ

As the late night passes
The River of Heaven
Shimmers on the surface
Of the flooded rice fields.   HIROSE IZEN

Spring night
A flute player
Passes by.   MASAOKA SHIKI

I can see the stones
On the bottom fluctuate
Through the clear water.   MASAOKA SHIKI

All the hot night
The quail
Sleepless in his cage.   MASAOKA SHIKI

The wild geese cry.
Below them on the reefs
The waves
White in the night.   MASAOKA SHIKI

Frozen in the ice
A maple leaf.   MASAOKA SHIKI

On the eve of death
The autumn cicada
Is noisier than ever.   MASAOKA SHIKI

Fresh from the Void
The moon
On the waves of the sea.   MASAOKA SHIKI

Shitting in the winter turnip field
The distant lights of the city.   MASAOKA SHIKI

Winter midnight
My voice does not
Sound like my own.   OTSUJI

Against far off snow mountains
Two crows are flying.   MURAKAMI KIJŌ

Roasting chestnuts
The terrorist's wife
Is so beautiful.   ISHII ROGETSU

NOTES

YAMABE AKAHITO, who lived in the middle of the eighth century, is one of the greatest poets of the *Manyōshū* anthology. Nobody knows what *"nubatama"* means — possibly "jet" — *"nuba"* is supposed to be a black fruit, and nobody knows what *"hisagi"* trees were either. Nevertheless the poem [1] is one of wholeness, harmony, and radiance, and shows why Akahito's short poems are ranked with Hitomaro's. There must be several thousand surviving screens and scrolls in which artists have rendered Akahito's cranes.

YOSANO AKIKO was born in 1878 in the family of Ōtori in the ancient merchant city of Sakai. In 1900 she went to Tokyo, studied poetry with Yosano Hiroshi, who considered himself the leader of the new poetry (*tanka*) movement, and soon married him. For a while, in Tokyo and Kyoto they were involved in a tragic *maison à trois*, with a young woman whom they both loved deeply. After a few years she died of tuberculosis. Akiko and Hiroshi founded the "New Poetry Society" and its organ, the magazine *Myōjō*, "Morning Star." Hiroshi always thought of himself as the genius of the family, although he was a sentimental and commonplace poet, who learned little from the French Symbolists whom he adored. Akiko was quickly recognized and soon earned enough money to send Hiroshi to Paris from 1911 to 1914, but she was only able to save enough money for herself to stay part of 1912, and members of her family assisted them both to return to Japan. She wrote many collections of poetry, novels, essays, children's stories, and fairy tales. She did a complete translation, of great beauty of style, of *The Tale of Genji* into modern Japanese. But the day before the manuscript was to go to the publisher, the great Tokyo earthquake of 1923 struck and all copies were destroyed. She bravely set to work and did it all over within the year. She was a leading feminist and pacifist and a socialist sympathizer. Her poem against the Russo-Japanese War was the first direct criticism of the Emperor ever printed except in political pamphlets, and she wrote in defense and in memoriam of the socialist and anarchist martyrs of 1912 whose execution shocked the world—much as did the Haymarket Martyrs and Sacco and Vanzetti.

She is the only truly great poet to write in traditional *tanka* form in modern times. She and Hiroshi thought of themselves as stylistic revolutionaries, but in fact her poems are full of echoes of the classics and some are deliberately modeled on well known *Manyōshū* poems. But then, behind every renascence of poetry in *tanka* form in Japan has lain a return to the purity of the *Manyō*. Akiko is more than this—she is one of the world's great women poets, comparable to Christina Rossetti, Gaspara Stampa, Louise Labé, and Li Ching Chao. She is certainly one of the very greatest poets of her time — the most perfect expression of the "Art Nouveau" sensibility — like Debussy, who should have set her poems to music.

She lived until 1942, productive to the end, having betimes in her literary career also mothered eleven children.

"*Koto no ne ni*" [III] echoes a *Manyōshū* poem in this book.

"*Kuro kami no*" [V], from her first book, *Midaregami*, culminates the long series, from Mikata and his wife, in the *Manyōshū*, of tangled hair poems.

"*Nagisa naru*" [IX] — another echo.

"*Michi o iwazu*" [XI] is as much a statement of a new concept of love as *The Doll's House*.

"*Ara iso ni*" [XII] is another echo. (See *100 Poems from the Japanese*.)

"*Yamadera no*" [XIII] refers to the frail temporary shelter in which ancient Japanese culminated marriage.

Kimi yuku to [XVI]: *shirahagi* is white bush clover — lespedeza.

Ki-nakanu wo [XVII]: the *ueguisu* is not a nightingale and does not sing at night. It is the Japanese bush warbler, a small, olive-green and brown bird with a beautiful song. (*Horeites cantans cantans*, or *Homochlamys cantans*.)

EIFUKU MON-IN (1271-1342) was the wife of the Emperor Fushimi. Her personal name was Akiko. *Kinu* means silk and *kinuginu* is an onomatopoeia for the silken rustling of trembling lovers. This is one of many *kinuginu* poems. It originally meant "dressing each other," parting on the morning of the first sexual meeting of lovers, but now means simply silk or dress.

KAKINOMOTO NO HITOMARO flourished in the later years of the seventh century and reputedly died in 739. He was probably a personal attendant of the Emperor Mommu (697-707) and later retired to Iwami where he may have been born, and died there, although his reputed tomb is at Ichii no Moto in Yamato. He is considered Japan's greatest poet and has provided models for countless poems since his time. Omi is the old name of Lake Biwa. These flower-gathering, dew-drenching poems so common in classic times have an erotic significance, as in Chinese.

ŌKURA ICHIJITSU. His dates are unknown, as are the original characters for his name. (The calligraphy used is that for "anonymous.")

IZUMI SHIKIBU (Shikibu is a title) was born in the last quarter of the tenth century and was a contemporary of Murasaki Shikibu, Sei Shōnagon, Ise Tayu, a group of great women writers unsurpassed in the history of any literature. Her story of one of her many love affairs, the *Izumi Shikibu Nikki*, is a masterpiece of Japanese prose. In spite of, or perhaps because of, her scandalous sex life, she seems to me to have the deepest, most poignant Buddhist sensibility of all the classical writers. Her daughter Koshikibu no Naishi was also a fine poet. *Iro* means color in every English metaphorical sense also.

FUJIWARA NŌ KAMATARI (614-69) was the founder of the great power of the Fujiwara clan. He was one of the assassins of the Sogas, father and son, who then dominated the Empress Kōgyoku, established the Emperor Kōtoku on the throne and inaugurated the Taiwa Reform, a revolutionary program modelled on China. Born Nakatomi nō Kamako, he was given the name Fujiwara and his family has remained powerful to this day, although they no longer rule behind the throne or routinely marry their daughters to Emperors and Crown Princes. *Etari* really means "done" her, which has the same sense as in English. He usually seems to have got whatever he wanted.

112

MINAMOTO NO KANEMASA lived in the twelfth century. *Awajishima* is my favorite Japanese poem and there is a long note on an earlier version in my *100 Poems from the Japanese* which explicates a few of the implicits. For that book I cut the note severely and now would like to add: *kayou* "goes in and out" or "back and forth," is also used as the Old Testament King James Version uses "he went in unto her" and here it especially means back and forth from rebirth to rebirth in the world of illusion — "*Yo no naka no*." Isanagi and Isanami descended from Heaven, danced around a kind of maypole or phallic pillar, had sex, and begot the islands of Japan. Awaji was the afterbirth of the first begetting — the land on which they stood was called *Ono-goro-jima*, as well as "never meeting" (or finding) which had dripped from the jewel spear of Heaven. Awaji can also be read as "my shame" but the Chinese characters used in the *Nihonshoki* mean "foam road." Awaji closes the eastern end of the Inland Sea, and Suma is four and a half miles west from the center of Kobe opposite the tip of the island. Here in the Shingon Temple Fukushōji (Sumadera) is enshrined the famous flute *Aoba no fue* of the young hero Taira no Atsumori who perished in the great battle with Yoshitsune's forces, and who is the subject of two of the greatest Noh plays. It should be borne in mind that Kanemasa lived in the time of the Taira-Minamoto wars, when men perished like bubbles and the dead were like flocks of sea birds, crying between the worlds. Due to pollution the chidori (shore birds) of Awaji are close to extinction and Suma beach cannot be swum in.

TAIRA NO KANEMORI lived in the tenth century. He was a great grandson of Prince Koretaka, a high courtier of the Emperors Murakami and Daigo, and governor of Echigo Province.

LADY KASA lived in the eighth century and was a lover of Yakamochi, to whom she wrote poems that show great passion and strength of character.

ONO NO KOMACHI (834-80) is the legendary beauty of Japan, comparable to the Chinese Yang Kuei-fei. She was the daughter of Yoshisada, Lord of Dewa. She is supposed to have died old, ugly and a beggar, but this is a legend, perpetuated by three of the finest Noh plays. She is certainly one of Japan's "six greatest poets." Her poems with their complex meanings are perfect examples of Empson's *Seven Types of Ambiguity*.

SAKANOE NO KORENORI lived in the tenth century.

SHAMI MANSEI flourished in the early eighth century. His lay name was Kasamaro. Governor of several provinces, he became a high court official and the next year became a monk. There is a slightly different version of this poem in the *Manyōshū*. (The name can also be spelled Manzei.) It is one of the earliest of the *Yo no naka no* (or *wo*) poems. The *Manyō* version:

> This world of ours
> To what shall I compare it?
> Put to sea in the morning,
> A boat which rowed away
> And left no track.

> *Yo no naka wo*
> *Nani ni tatoemu*
> *Asaboraki*
> *Kogi-inishi fune no*
> *Ato naki ga goto*

Asaborake in the *Shūi Shu* means "at early dawn"; "*Ato no shiranami*" — its track on the white waves" and also, "its track unknown."

MARICHIKO is the pen name of a contemporary young woman who lives near the temple of Marishi-ben in Kyoto. Marishi-ben is an Indian, pre-Aryan, goddess of the dawn who is a bodhisattva in Buddhism and patron of geisha, prostitutes, women in childbirth and lovers. Few temples or shrines to her or even statues exist in Japan, but her presence is indicated by statues, often in avenues like sphinxes, of wild boars, who draw her chariot. She has three faces: the front of compassion; one side, a sow; the other a woman in orgasm. She is a popular, though hidden deity of tantric, Tachigawa Shingon, and as the Light of Lights, the *shakti*, the Power of Bliss of

Vairocana (the primordial Buddha, Dainichi Nyorai), seated on his lap in sexual bliss.

MIKATA SHAMI may have been Yamada Mikata who flourished in the seventh-eighth century, possibly a contemporary of Hitomaro. He also wrote some Chinese poems. This exchange with his wife is the beginning of the long series of *midaregami*, tangled hair, poems which culminate in Yosano Akiko's first book.

LADY SONO NO OMI IKUHA. Nothing is known of her except that she was Mikata's wife and Sono Ikuha's daughter.

ŌSHIKOCHI NO MITSUNE lived in the tenth century. He was one of the compilers of the second great anthology — after the *Manyōshū* — the *Kokinshu*, which introduced a new, softer, more subtle sensibility. Although he never rose to high rank, he was an important poet.

THE MONK NŌIN (998-1050), born Tachibana no Nagayasu, was a minor official before he became a monk. He was also a critic and theorist of poetics.

FUJIWARA NO OKIKAZE lived in the tenth century. He was one of the first, with his Hamanari System, to begin the formularization of verse.

OYAKEME, A GIRL OF BUZEN. Nothing is known of her. Her poem appears in the *Manyōshū* in a group of otherwise unknown young women.

SAIGYŌ (1118-90) was descended from the Fujiwara. His secular name was Sāto Norikyo. He was a favorite of the ex-Emperor Toba and a famous archer. At twenty-three he left his wife and children and became a monk and travelled throughout Japan reciting poetry and preaching. He inaugurates with Shunzei and Teika a new phase of the Japanese poetic sensibility.

ONOE NO SHIBAFUNE (Saishu) (1876-?) was a leading Taisho (early twentieth-century) poet and a professor of Japanese classical literature.

FUJIWARA NO SUEYOSHI (1152-1211) The plovers grow closer wing to wing until they approach the mythical Chinese love birds who share a wing between them. "As the tide of illusion rises and the Buddha Law sinks toward the Age of Darkness the migrating creatures, crying with pain, draw closer and more dependent on each other." The Buddhist symbolism resembles that of *Awajishima*.

ŌTOMO NO TABITO (665-731) belonged to the Otomo clan, one of the most powerful family groups of the seventh-eighth centuries. He was the father of the great poet Ōtomo Yakamochi and Governor of Kyushu, Grand Councilor of State, and a general. His series of poems in praise of sake are still sung, but his poems of loneliness and loss of his beloved wife are actually his best.

FUJIWARA NO TEIKA (Sadai-e) (1162-1241) was the son of the poet Toshinari. He was involved in the gathering of the *Shin Kokinshu* and the *Hyakunin Isshu* (*100 Poems of 100 Poets*, played as a card game to this day) and author of the introduction to *Superior Poems of Our Time* (*Kindai Shuka*), a critical landmark in the history of Japanese poetics. He and the poets associated with his poetics altered the course of Japanese poetry and changed the poetic sensibility. He is one of the major Japanese poets, though often considered decadent by the followers of the pure *Manyōshū* tradition. His most poignant love poems were written, as was *Hajime yori*, to young girls in his old age. "The floating bridge of dreams" [LIV] echoes the title of the last book of the *Genji Monogatori*, but Murasaki herself echoes earlier poems. Perhaps Teika was the last truly major tanka poet, until Yosano Akiko. Hundreds of paintings, and now, photographs, have been made of poem LII.

THE EMPEROR TENCHI (also spelled Tenji) was traditionally the thirty-eighth Emperor of Japan (662-71). He published an extensive, for Japan, law code, was an able administrator, and withdrew all Japanese forces from the unprofitable occupation of Korea.

FUJIWARA NO TOSHINARI (Shunzei) (1114-1204), father of Teika, was, with his son and Saigyō, one of the principal leaders of the twelfth-thirteenth century "revolution of the sensibility." He was also a famous painter and calligrapher. He became a Shinto priest in later life. *Yu sareba* [LVII] is a favorite subject for two-leaf screens for the winter season.

KI NO TSURAYUKI (882-946) is a major poet of his period. He was general editor of the second anthology, the *Kokinshu*, and wrote for it a famous critical preface which founded Japanese poetic aesthetics and which is still taught as a masterpiece of early prose. He compiled another anthology, the *Shinsen Shu*, and a selection from the *Manyōshū*. He also wrote the *Tosa Nikki*, the *Tosa Diary*, of a journey from Tosa where he had been Governor, back to the capital — another masterpiece of early prose. Tsurayuki, his son Tokibuni, Tomonori, Mitsune, Tadamine, and the others associated with the compiling of the *Kokinshu* are the first clearly defined "school" in Japanese poetry. He was also famed as a calligrapher. Japanese still gather a *bouquet garni* of certain pungent herbs as their first shoots come through the soil, make a strong tea, mix it with sweet sake and drink it on New Year's Day. Since the six-weeks-later lunar New Year has been abandoned, the sake companies give away little packets of dry herbs during the last week of December. "Gathering young herbs" is a cliché for spending a night with girl entertainers and courtesans — later with geisha.

ŌTOMO NO YAKAMOCHI (718-85) was the eldest son of Tabito. He, Hitomaro, Akahito and Okura are considered the leading poets of the *Manyōshū* and amongst the greatest in Japan of all time. He held many high offices of state, as well as General of the Eastern Armies, a position that would in later centuries become *Shogun* and lead to the governorship of Japan until the nineteenth century. After his death, due to the crime of a remote and minor member of the family, the Ōtomo clan was broken up and became extinct, to be revived in the eleventh century. "*Ime no ai wa*" [LX] is the first of many poems, including contemporary geisha songs, that say essentially the same thing. Lady Sakanoe was an aunt and lover of Yakamochi.

SONE NO YOSHITADA (late tenth century) was Vice-Lord of Tango, one of the leading poets of the medieval age, and, says Miyamori Asatarō, "a haughty, narrow minded, eccentric man." Nevertheless he was a considerable poet.

PRINCE YUHARA (eighth century) was a grandson of Emperor Tenchi. His few love poems are amongst the most touching and personal of the early *Manyōshū*.

FUJIWARA NO YOSHIFUSA (804-872) was Minister of the Right, Prime Minister, and Regent from 858 to 872. His daughter Akiko became the wife and Empress of Emperor Montoku and the poem is to her. The original says "beautiful flower" rather than "flower like beauty." Under Yoshifusa and Akiko the power and wealth of the Fujiwara clan greatly increased.

ANONYMOUS. I have grouped the anonymous poems from the classic anthologies together and all others, regardless of period, together. Many of these, both early and later, are folksongs, though some have been reworked by literary poets, as in the Chinese *Shi Ching* — *The Book of Songs;* others are literary imitations of folksong — like the Chinese Six Dynasties *Yueh chih*; others are simply by unknown authors. But the general feeling is certainly folkloristic. Many *dodoitsu* and *sedoka* are relatively modern geisha songs which directly echo famous classic poems.

"*Asagumori*" is usually thought to be to a dead prince lamented by a Palace guard. But I think this was a poem to a dead or departed lover.

"*Ashidama mo*" is a seventh night of the seventh moon poem, though supposed to be written earlier in the year. On the festival of Tanabata the Cowboy (Altair) crosses the River of Heaven (The Milky Way) to lie for one night only with his lover, the Weaver Girl (Vega). He crosses by a bridge of magpies with linked wings, or, in some versions, by a boat or a raft. The Festival and legend are widespread in the East and are comparable to the Hebrew Festival of Succoth, which was accompanied with lines of girls and young men dancing on opposite sides of running water — preferably a newly opened irrigation channel — and culminating in an *heirosgamos* (Sholomo and the Shulamite in the *Song of Songs*) and followed by group marriage. The ceremony

118

still survives in Indochina, especially Laos, and in remote villages in Taiwan and Japan. Tanabata is still, even in Tokyo, a major festival. In Japan such group courtship songs are called *uta-gaki*. See Granet's *Danses et Legendes Anciennes de la Chine* and *Fêtes et Chansons Anciennes de la Chine*.

"*Shoji no futatsu*" is probably the strongest Buddhist poem in the *Manyōshū* and certainly exceptional for its time. It sounds like Izumi Shikibu.

In "*Ikahoro no*" *sane* and less *saneteba* are supposed to be noun and verb forms of *ne* — "sleep" — as euphemisms for sex, prefixed with the honorary *sa*. So the line would read "honorably sleep the honorable sleep with you." If so, this is a most atypical hapax. *Sane* means the clitoris, and the tongue, *saneteba*, means "I want to tongue." This interpretation gives nice scholars fits.

"*Komochiyama*" means Child Bearing Mountain. An *uta-gaki*? The poem is full of double meanings and may have arisen in the same group marriage rite as the Tanibata songs.

"*Ashi no ha ni*": these frontier guards were posted along the Eastern (actually Northeastern) lines against the aborigines, in *Manyō* times in the vicinity of Tokyo, or even further South, and in Kyushu.

"*Koto toreba*" is the model for Yosano Akiko's poem in this book. "Secluded" is better than "hidden" — it is as though in death his wife had secluded herself from this troubled world as a nun, but still, when touched by him, cried out.

"*Kazahaya no*" is obviously a folksong. *Kazahaya*, Windy Beach, is a proper name. It is still windy.

"*Yo no naka no* (or *wo*)" is one of many thousands of similar poems. I once thought of doing a small book of them from earliest times to a modern pop tune but gave up, surfeited. From this sentiment comes the later *Ukiyo* which reaches its height in Genroku, the golden age of the Tokugawa pleasure cities. Notice the sharp turn toward Buddhist sentiment in the *Kokinshū* as compared with the *Manyōshū*.

"*Nagarete wa*": Imo Mountain and Mount Se. "Big Brother and Little Sister," terms of endearment between lovers or husband and wife. Again, possibly originating in group marriage dance across water. There actually are such hills.

"*Yuki yaranu*": Sorry, but I have forgotten who wrote this poem. It is full of double meanings which take off from *yuki* which also means "snow."

"*Shio no mitsu*" is quoted by Sei Shōnagon in her *Pillow Book* as a very old folksong.

"*Shinonome no*" is another *kinuginu* poem.

A farmer's song.

"*Mime de kurushiki*" and the next six poems are *dodoitsu*; so they are probably entertainer's songs — but they sound literary in origin.

"*Natsu no yūbe wa*": I translated this in my adolescence. I have no idea where I got it. It sounds like a geisha song from Uji. "The lights of the boats" would be the torches of cormorant fishing boats.

"*Yume de wa nai ka to*" and the poem following it are *dodoitsu* on classical *tanka* models.

"*Kane ga naru ka ye*" is a song of the pleasure cities, with both a Buddhist and an erotic meaning.

"*Hototogisu kata*" and the poem following it are modelled on several classic *tanka*. The Japanese cuckoo does not say "cuckoo" — but something like its name — *hototogisu*.

"*Hitori neru yo wa*" is a prostitute's song from Yokohama.

"*Oki chidori no*" is an answer to the preceding *dodoitsu*.

"*Hito wa dono yo ni*" answers "*Oki chidori no*."